Dear ....,

You are invited to join us on a VIP tour of the ballet theater. We will take you behind the scenes, where you will discover everything that goes into one of our magical productions. You will be able to access all areas and watch our talented dancers, choreographers, musicians, designers, and technicians as they prepare for our latest ballet. After your tour, we invite you to the royal box to watch a performance of *Swan Lake*.

We look forward to welcoming you.

The Ballet Company

Written by

Charlotte Guillain

Illustrated by

Helen Shoesmith

WELBECK
EDITIONS

Welcome to the Theater

You can leave your coat in the cloakroom here in the entrance hall. Help yourself to a floor plan of the theater —it will help you find your way around. The box office is where people go to buy tickets to see a performance. You can also buy refreshments and programs here.

Let's begin the tour!

BOX OFFICE

CLOAKROOM

BALCONY

BAR

Contents

In the Auditorium

Let's start our tour in the auditorium, where the audience sits to experience the sights and sounds of a ballet. Over 2,000 people can sit in here to watch a performance.

Upstairs is the balcony, where the seats look down on the stage.

The royal box has the best seats in the house. It's where members of the royal family and other important people sit when they come to watch a performance.

The orchestra pit is just below the stage so the musicians are near the dancers as they play but are mostly out of sight. We'll take a closer look at this later.

If you look up at the back of the theater, you'll see the lighting booth. From here, engineers watch the performance so they can change the lighting effects on the stage at exactly the right moment.

The stalls are the seats that are just below or at the same level as the stage. All of the seats in the theater are angled and raked toward the stage so that everyone in the audience can see all of the dancers' bodies as they move.

The boxes sit to the sides of the stage and are separate spaces for five or six people. The boxes have special chairs and give a unique view of the dancing below.

The stage is at the front of the auditorium, in the center.

This designer is making sure Cinderella's ball dress fits perfectly. The gown needs to look extra special but the dancer needs to be able to move freely when she wears it. The skirt of this ball dress has three layers of net. The bodice is covered in embroidery, which is all done by hand. The dancer who is playing the part of Cinderella needs to be able to change into this dress in just a few minutes during a performance.

Costumes can be decorated in different ways. This designer is hand painting the prince's jacket to make sure there is lots of detail. Cinderella's crystal slippers are covered in intricate embroidery and jewels and diamonds to look extra special.

The Costume Department

This is the costume department. Every outfit for each ballet is designed, created, and looked after here. These talented wardrobe designers are working on the many beautiful costumes for *Cinderella*.

The Cinderella Story

This ballet was written by the Russian composer, Sergei Prokofiev. In this well-known story, Cinderella is treated like a servant by her stepmother and her daughters. When the prince invites them to a ball, Cinderella's stepmother rips up her invitation but her fairy godmother uses magic to send Cinderella to the palace. She dances with the prince but then runs away before midnight strikes, leaving one of her crystal slippers behind. The prince searches for Cinderella and finally declares his love for her.

All of the costumes need to be cleaned, ironed, and mended after each performance. Then they are hung carefully on a rail so every dancer and the dressers who help them know where to find their clothes.

This costume designer is making sketches for the next ballet that the company will perform.

This tutu is made from a fabric called tulle. It's designed to show the full length of a ballerina's legs and is made up of as many as 16 layers to give it a full shape. A special tutu can take as long as 60 hours to make.

Bodice

Basque

Skirt

The Shoe Room

This is the ballet company's shoe room. Every dancer has their own specially-made shoes stored on the shelves here. The ballet shoe manager's job is to check every ballerina's pointe shoes fit properly and to make sure each dancer has a steady supply of the right shoes. There are thousands of shoes in this room.

Pointe shoes are what female dancers wear when they perform. They make a ballerina's legs look longer and give them a lightness as they dance. Dancing on their toes makes ballerinas look delicate, almost as if they are floating. In fact, dancers need very strong legs and feet to be able to dance on pointe.

Pointe shoes have a sturdy and densely packed platform in the toe made from layers of fabric and paper hardened by glue, which the dancer balances on as they dance. The rest of the shoe is made of leather and cotton and is covered in shiny satin. There's no left and right—both shoes in a pair are identical.

The male dancers' shoes are flat and usually black. They are like a snug slipper with a soft, bendy sole that allows them to leap and land again easily.

Ballerinas spend a lot of time making their pointe shoes just right for their feet. They might darn the tips of their shoes to make them tougher, or file the soles to make them less slippery. Dancers sew elastic onto their shoes to keep them on, as well as the ribbons that they tie above their ankle bones to hold the shoes in place.

Pointe shoes don't last very long. A dancer can get through at least six pairs in a week!

13

Morning Ballet Class

All the dancers in the company have gathered in this large rehearsal studio for their morning ballet class. They do this class every morning for over an hour, six days a week, to warm up their bodies so they are flexible and ready for the rest of the day. The morning class also builds strength and improves the dancers' technique.

Fifth position

After a short warm-up routine, the dancers practice every technical exercise they might use in a ballet. They line up at a rail called the barre wearing flat shoes and repeat each position and movement over and over again. They wear legwarmers and other warm clothes while their muscles are starting to work.

Fourth position

Third position

Demi plié

Second position

First position

The ballet mistress leads the class, calling out which exercise the dancers are to move onto next. She moves around the room, correcting the dancers' movements and helping them to improve on technique. There are mirrors on the walls so the dancers can check their positions, and that they are moving correctly.

After working at the barre, the dancers practice larger movements without support in the center of the studio. The ballerinas put on their pointe shoes for this and work on the skills they need to balance, jump, and twirl on pointe. The male dancers work hard on their spins, leaps, and landings. By the end of the class, the dancers are performing their biggest jumps and most impressive pirouettes.

Grand jeté

The dancers always perform their morning class to music. A pianist comes every day to play live with them. There's a piano in the corner of every studio.

Pirouette

Entrechat

Sauté

Arabesque

15

The Rehearsal Studio

After the morning class, the dancers go to rehearsals for the rest of the day. Even if they are performing in the evening, they will rehearse for hours during the day before going on stage. In this studio, two of the company's principal dancers are rehearsing their scenes from *The Firebird*.

The Firebird Story

The Firebird was composed by the Russian-born composer Igor Stravinsky. In this ballet, a prince captures a magical bird. To persuade him to release her, the bird gives the prince one of her feathers and promises to come if he ever needs her help. When the prince discovers a group of princesses trapped under an evil magician's spell, he calls for the Firebird to help defeat the villain. The princesses are set free, the prince marries one of them, and everyone is happy.

The dancers are working with the choreographer. His job is to arrange the dance steps and sequences of movement for this ballet. He is watching carefully as the dancers rehearse and he demonstrates sections of the dance to help them improve.

The rehearsal room is the same size as the stage in the auditorium, so the dancers know exactly where they need to be at all times. During rehearsal, a pianist plays the music from the ballet that the orchestra will be playing in the performances.

The ballerina is wearing a tutu and headdress here so both she and her partner will be used to making their movements when she dances in full costume.

The Healthcare Suite

Welcome to the healthcare suite. This studio is vital for all dancers, whether they want to maintain their strength and avoid physical problems or if they need treatment for injuries.

This dancer is lifting weights in the gym to strengthen specific muscles and recover from a hip injury. Dancers can become injured through falls and accidents and also through fatigue and overuse of certain muscles. Working in the healthcare suite can help dancers to avoid injury and have a long and healthy career.

This gyrotonic equipment helps dancers to lengthen and tone up their muscles and explore a wide range of movements in their body.

When a male dancer is preparing for a key role in a ballet where he has to lift his partner a lot, he'll visit the suite to build up his strength by lifting weights and improve his balance with Pilates exercises.

In the rehabilitation studio, a physical therapist is treating an injured dancer on the massage table. She'll give the dancer specific strengthening exercises to repeat in the healthcare suite so she can eventually start to train safely again.

Experts in the healthcare suite can help dancers with their mental health so they can cope with the stress of performing at such a high level. Dancers can also get advice on the nutritious diet they need to be healthy and strong and to give them the energy to rehearse and perform for hours every day.

The Dancers' Canteen

After all that hard work, the dancers need to refuel. This is the company's canteen, where everyone who works in the ballet theater can meet to relax, catch up with friends, and eat.

Dancers use up a lot of energy in the morning ballet class and their rehearsals. Some of them might be performing on stage later, too. So, they need the right food and drink to get them through to the end of the evening.

The water fountain is where dancers can refill their water bottles so they can rehydrate after all the physical exertion and sweating in the morning.

Ballet dancers need to eat food that is easy to digest and which can slowly release the energy they need throughout the day. Food that is rich in carbohydrates, such as pasta, bread, rice, and fresh fruit is important. Dancers also need to have plenty of light snacks, such as bananas, nuts, fruit smoothies, or rice cakes at hand throughout the day for a quick energy boost whenever they need it. Most dancers try to avoid refined sugar as it doesn't give them the long-lasting energy they need.

Milk and yogurt are good sources of calcium which is vital for keeping dancers' bones healthy and strong.

Protein is an important part of a dancer's diet as it helps to build and repair muscle. In the canteen there is plenty of tuna, chicken, beans, and tofu to provide this nutrient.

Eating all the right amounts of vitamins and minerals helps to keep dancers healthy and able to perform at the best of their ability.

Relaxing with friends is as important as eating well. Everyone needs a break and a chat before going back to work.

The Christmas tree in the ballet is seen to grow during the transformation scene in the middle of the performance. This tree is made of plywood and is placed on a lifting platform below the stage. When the platform rises up, it looks as if the tree is growing before the audience's eyes.

The stage for a ballet needs to have a sprung floor so the dancers can leap high and land safely without getting injured. The set is extremely lightweight so it doesn't weigh down the sprung dance floor. The way designers paint the sets can make them look realistic and much heavier than they really are.

The Set-building Workshop

Welcome to the workshop where the sets are built for each ballet. The designers here are busy preparing the set for *The Nutcracker*, a favorite ballet at Christmas.

The Nutcracker Story

The Nutcracker was written by the Russian composer Pyotr Tchaikovsky. In this story, a girl named Clara is given a magical nutcracker for Christmas by her godfather. When midnight chimes, the Christmas tree grows, toys and animals come to life, and Clara is transported to the Land of Snow, where her nutcracker turns into a prince. Together they travel to the Land of Sweets before Clara returns home and wakes up beside the Christmas tree.

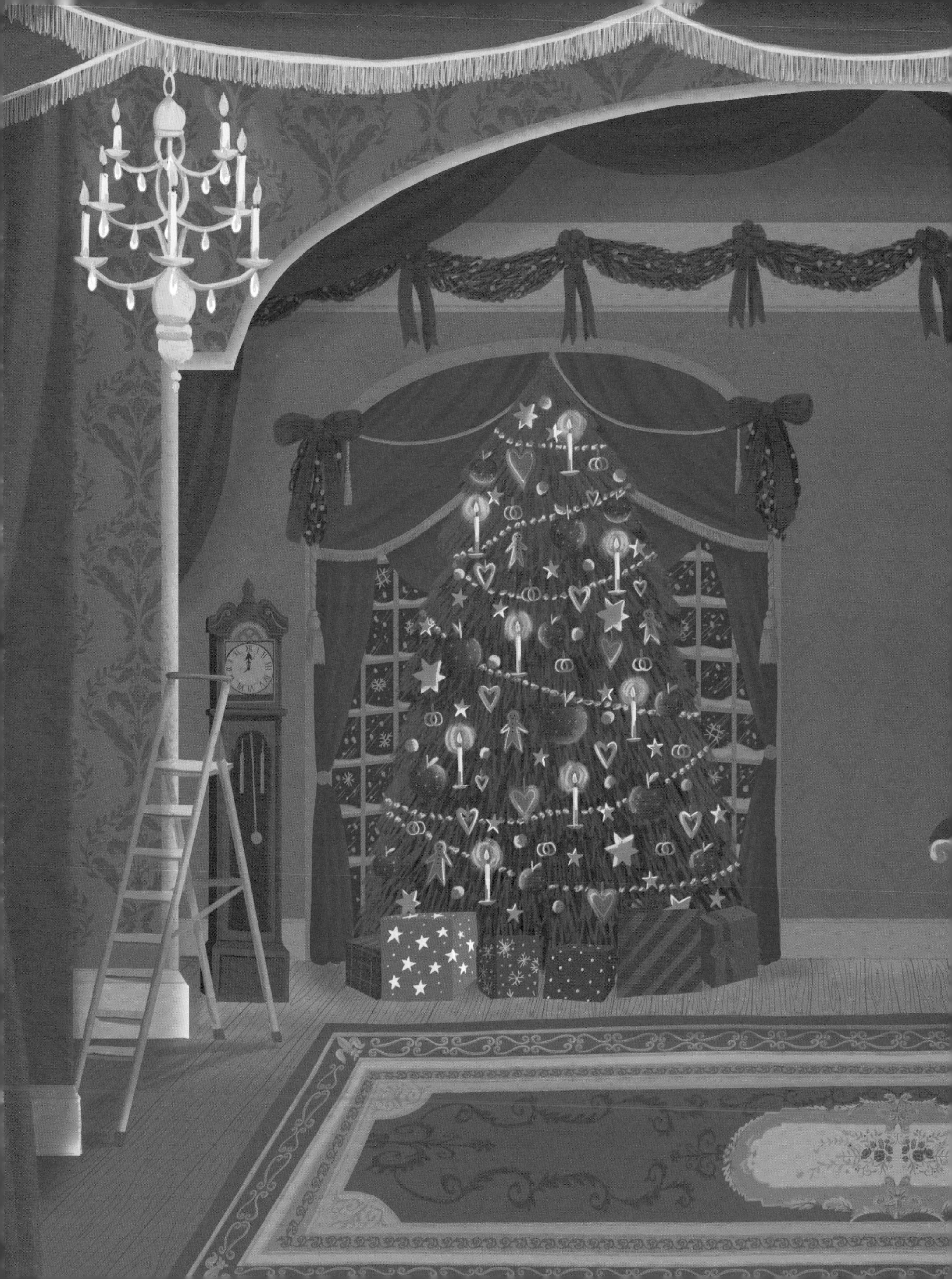

Set-builders have a range of practical skills to build and decorate beautiful scenery effectively. They need great problem-solving skills to find clever special effects for each ballet.

The set on a ballet doesn't take up too much space on the stage. This is so the dancers have as much room as possible to move.

The scenery at the back of the stage is hand-painted onto huge backcloths. These scenes can look very striking.

This long bag has holes in it. It's filled with fake snow and hung on long bars, high above the stage. When the dancers perform the snowflake dance in the Land of Snow, the bag is moved so the fake snow falls through the holes and it looks like it's snowing on the stage.

The Lighting Department

This is the lighting department. All of the lighting equipment that the company needs for its different productions is found here. Lighting designers and technicians are based here but during performances you'll find them working in the lighting booth that you saw at the back of the auditorium.

These rows of shelves are full of carefully stacked and labeled lights, filters, and cables. There are over 3,000 electric lights stored here. The lighting engineers know exactly where to find each piece of equipment when it's needed.

The lighting designer has worked with the director to plan how the lights can be used to create amazing colors and effects on stage. She is using computer software here to show how the stage will look with each lighting change. The people who design the sets and costumes need to have this overview so they know everything will look perfect together. As the sets in a ballet are not very big or complicated, the lights play an important part in setting the scene.

Lighting effects, along with the music, can help create the right mood at different points during a performance. The lighting technicians need to follow the dancers' movements and the music to make sure the timing of the lighting changes is exactly right.

When the theater is set up for a new ballet, the engineers will take the lighting that's needed and set it up on rigs high above the stage. There are five bars above the stage for the lights to be fixed onto and each can hold around half a million pounds' worth of lights.

The Makeup Studio

The dancers need to put special stage makeup on before a performance so their faces are clearly visible in the bright lights. In the makeup studio they can find everything they need.

Most dancers apply their own makeup before going on stage. They start with a base layer all over their face. This needs to stay put once they start to move and sweat. Dancers need to remember to put this base makeup on their ears and neck, too, so they match the rest of their face under the lights.

Makeup is used to make the dancers' cheekbones and lips stand out. A highlighting powder helps to make the dancer's features glow under the lights on stage.

It's important for dancers to make their eyes look bigger so the audience can see their faces clearly from all around the auditorium. They make their eyebrows darker and more defined and then emphasize their eyes using dark eyeshadows and long false eyelashes. A white eyeliner can also make the eyes look larger and wide open.

When a dancer needs a more complicated makeup design, a makeup artist applies the makeup. They might use face paints and sparkling glitter, too. Some classic ballet characters are magical or wicked and need special exaggerated features. Makeup artists will often use prosthetics, for example false noses and chins. The prosthetic is carefully stuck onto the dancer's face with a special glue. It's important that it doesn't fall off in the middle of a dance. Then the makeup artist uses makeup to blend the prosthetic in with the rest of the dancer's face.

The Wig Room

This is the wig room. All of the wigs used by the company during performances are specially made here and carefully looked after by the technicians.

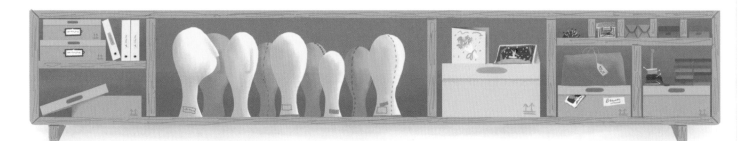

These wigs are ready for a performance of *Sleeping Beauty*, by Tchaikovsky. There are many fairy tale characters in this ballet so some colorful and elaborate wigs are needed. Ballet dancers often wear wigs as it makes it much easier to change their look and style on stage.

The Sleeping Beauty Story

This ballet tells the story of the baby Princess Aurora, who is cursed by an evil fairy. When Aurora is 16 years old, she pricks her finger on a spindle and falls asleep for 100 years. The good Lilac Fairy makes the whole kingdom fall asleep too, until a prince awakens Aurora with a kiss. They are married and live happily ever after.

Each wig is made to fit perfectly on a dancer's head. The wig maker makes a mold of each dancer's head and then makes a net cap. Then they add every individual hair by hand before styling and decorating the wig. It can take up to 60 hours to add all the hair to one wig.

The wigs need to be stored carefully on wooden head shapes and after each performance they are checked, brushed, and restyled as necessary.

When a dancer is ready to wear their wig, they come to the wig room with their hair tied up in a bun and a thin stocking cap is put over their head. Then the wig is placed over the top and fixed in place with hair grips and special wig glue so it will not slip.

Wig makers also make beards and moustaches for the male dancers.

The Orchestra Pit

We're back in the auditorium now, where the orchestra is working hard on a rehearsal in the orchestra pit. The company usually performs two ballets alternately. This is called repertory. The orchestra is practicing the music for the ballet *Romeo and Juliet*, which will be performed tomorrow.

The orchestra usually practices together in a studio but they run through the music in the orchestra pit for their last two rehearsals before a new performance. The conductor is taking the musicians through the music very carefully so that everything will be perfect.

There are lots of famous pieces of music in this ballet, such as the dramatic "Dance of the Knights" and the romantic "Balcony Scene."

The Romeo and Juliet Story

The music for *Romeo and Juliet* was composed by Prokofiev. This ballet tells the tragic story of two young lovers, who fall in love despite coming from families that are sworn enemies. They get married and try to be together but when Romeo's friend and Juliet's cousin are killed, Romeo is banished and Juliet's parents tell her she must marry a nobleman, Paris. Instead, Juliet pretends to kill herself and sends a message to Romeo. Unfortunately, Romeo thinks Juliet is really dead and he kills himself. When Juliet finds his lifeless body, she also takes her own life.

The music for this ballet includes some unusual instruments, such as a tenor saxophone and mandolins, which you can see here.

The group of musicians in the pit isn't a full-size orchestra but they're still squashed in tightly. They have downward-facing lights on their music stands so they can read the music without distracting the dancers or audience.

In the Wings

The rehearsals are over, the dancers are in their costumes, wigs, and makeup and they're starting to gather backstage, waiting for the performance to begin.

Five minutes before the performance starts, which is called the "beginners' call," the dancers who will be first onstage move to the wings at the side of the stage. They will have done a warm-up class earlier, repeating the same sort of exercises they did in their morning ballet class. Now they need to make sure their muscles keep warm and their body is ready to face the physical challenges of dancing on stage. They stretch to keep mobile and to calm their nerves before the ballet starts.

The dancers listen to the orchestra warming up and start to focus on the dancing that lies ahead. They are feeling excited and nervous as they hear the chattering of the audience and a bell ringing to tell people to take their seats.

Rosin box

It can be quite a squash in the wings as there are so many dancers in *Swan Lake*. The dancers who perform in the *corps de ballet* as a group behind the soloist and principal dancers need to get organized into the right order to dance onto stage. The stage manager checks to make sure everyone is where they need to be.

At last, the orchestra finishes tuning up and a hush falls over the audience. The lights in the auditorium dim and the dancers take one last deep breath. The ballet is about to begin.

The final touches are made to costumes and a hair technician might straighten out a wig or two. Ballerinas dip their pointe shoes (and sometimes their feet) in the rosin box to prevent any slips on stage. Rosin is made from a tree resin and comes in rock form, which is crushed into a dusty powder. They also check that the ribbons and elastics on their shoes are firmly tied and tucked away nicely. Stage hands bring props to dancers who need them.

The music for this ballet was written by Tchaikovsky and much of it has become very well known. You have probably heard the "Swan Theme" and the "Dance of the Cygnets" before.

Two of the best dancers in the company are dancing the part of Odette and Siegfried. These exceptional performers are named principal dancers and will have rehearsed their parts for hours every day for weeks.

On the stage

The curtain is up, the lights in the theater have darkened, and the orchestra is playing—the ballet has begun. All the rehearsals, costumes, lighting, set design, makeup, and music have come together ready for the dancers to perform *Swan Lake*.

The Swan Lake Story

This ballet tells the story of Prince Siegfried, who comes across a flock of swans while he is hunting. One of them turns into a beautiful maiden named Odette. She tells him that all of the swans have been transformed by an evil spell performed by the wicked sorcerer, Von Rothbart. Siegfried and Odette fall in love but at dawn she becomes a swan again. Back at the palace, the sorcerer disguises his daughter Odile as Odette and Siegfried says he will marry her before realizing he has been tricked. Now he will never break the spell. Odette forgives him but chooses to die rather than be a swan forever. Siegfried leaps into the lake with her and their deaths release the other swans from the spell.

The ballerinas playing the large group of swans are called the *corps de ballet*. They have to work well as a team and be perfectly coordinated and precise. They move their arms together so gracefully to give the idea of a flock of swans flying.

The same dancer who plays Odette changes into a black tutu to play Odile later in the ballet. At one point, she will have to perform 32 quick spins called *fouettes* in succession.

After the Performance

When the dancers reach the end of the ballet, the music stops, the lights on the stage go dark, and the curtain closes. Then suddenly there is a rush of noise, as the audience gets to their feet, clapping and cheering.

As the curtains open again, the stage is lit brightly as the dancers run back on stage to take the applause. They have practiced the bows that they make at the end of the performance as carefully as every other move. First the members of the *corps de ballet* bow together in a group, followed by soloists. Then the principal dancers who played the main roles come to the stage individually to bow slowly and gracefully.

The dancers may be called back several times for applause. Sometimes the choreographer is brought onto the stage so the audience can clap for them, too. The conductor turns to bow and the orchestra stands to receive their applause.

Bouquets of roses are presented to the principal ballerinas, the conductor, and the choreographer. People sitting at the front of the auditorium can also throw flowers onto the stage to show their appreciation.

Finally, the curtain closes and the audience begins to chatter and move out of the auditorium. The ballet is over but the whole room is buzzing with an excitement and appreciation that follows the crowd out of the theater and into the city street outside.

45

In the Dressing Room

Behind the curtain, the dancers leave the stage and hurry to their dressing rooms. They congratulate each other on a wonderful performance as they remove their pointe shoes and begin to stretch out, cool down their muscles, and slow their heart rate down after so much physical work.

While the principal dancers have their own dressing rooms, most of the other dancers share rooms to get ready in before a performance and to get changed afterward. They need to drink plenty of water now to rehydrate as they will have sweated and used a lot of energy on the stage.

Some dancers need to put their feet in an ice bath to help relieve any soreness and help their feet to recover more quickly. Many dancers lie on the floor and raise their legs against the wall. This helps avoid swelling in their legs and ankles. They massage their tired muscles, too.

The dancers chat to each other and start to relax as they remove their thick stage makeup and any wigs, beards, or false eyelashes. They carefully remove their costumes and hang them up, ready for the wardrobe department to check, clean, and iron for the next performance. Then it's time for a warm shower.

At the Stage Door

When the dancers have changed, they are finally ready to leave the theater. It may be over 12 hours since they arrived earlier in the day for their warm-up and morning ballet class.

After the physical demands of a ballet performance, dancers can be tired and hungry and will soon need a light meal full of protein and carbohydrates to help them recover. Then it will be time to head home, relax, and go to sleep so they are ready for tomorrow's morning class, rehearsals, and another performance.

It's time to leave the theater now. Which ballet would you like to come and see the dancers perform next?